7th June 04

ALL WAYS OF LOOKING AT

WEATHER

JANE WALKER

GLOUCESTER PRESS
LONDON • NEW YORK • SYDNEY

INTRODUCTION

©
Aladdin Books Ltd 1994

Designed and produced by
Aladdin Books Ltd
28 Percy Street
London W1P 9FF

First published in
Great Britain in 1994 by
WATTS BOOKS
96 Leonard Street
London EC2A 4RH

Design: David West
             Children's Book
             Design
Designer: Flick Killerby

Editor: Angela Travis

Illustrator: Ian Thompson
Cartoons: Tony Kenyon

Consultant: Joyce Pope

ISBN 0 7496 1700 4

From bright sunshine to dark cloudy skies, from heavy rain to freezing cold, the weather affects us all each day. In this book you can find out what makes the weather, and why it is always changing. Take a look at extreme weather conditions and how people cope with them. You can discover a lot of **Amazing Facts** about weather and have fun with **Practical Projects** and your own **Weather Diary.**

CONTENTS

WHAT IS THE WEATHER?

The weather can be hot or cold, wet or dry, windy or still. All our weather is caused by changes in the air around the Earth as the air heats up and cools down. Weather plays a very important part in our daily lives. Will it be sunny or cloudy today? Will it snow tomorrow? Bad weather can stop trains from running and aeroplanes from taking off, destroy crops and stop work outdoors.

Weather protection

We often need protection from the weather. When it's very sunny, we wear sunhats, sunglasses and use suncream. In the rain, we wear raincoats, boots and use umbrellas. In the cold, people wear thick clothes to keep warm.

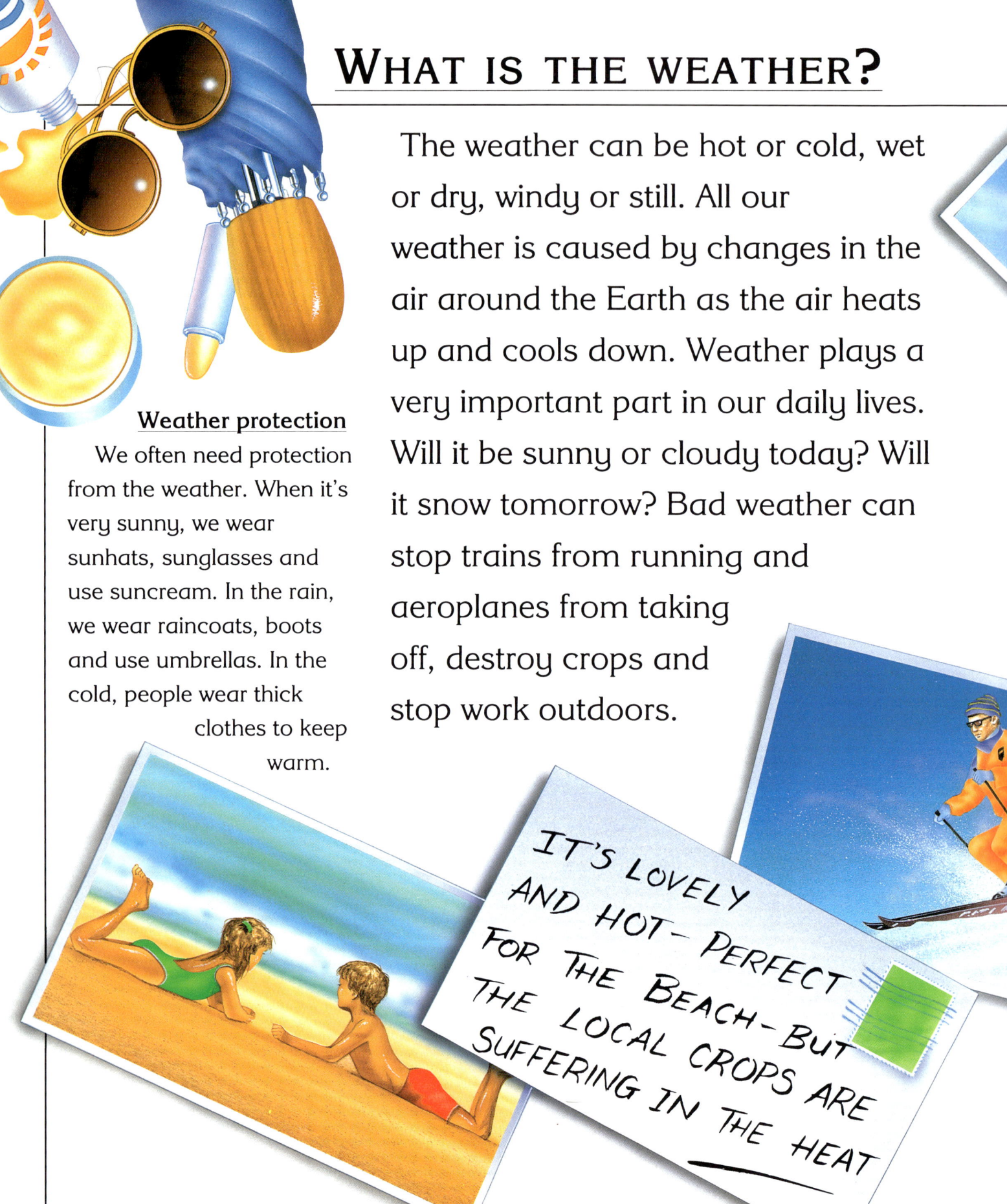

IT'S LOVELY AND HOT – PERFECT FOR THE BEACH – BUT THE LOCAL CROPS ARE SUFFERING IN THE HEAT

Because the MOON is outside the Earth's atmosphere it has no weather.

As the water vapour in the air cools, it changes into drops of water and forms clouds. The water drops fall to the ground as RAIN.

TEMPERATURE is the heat of the air around us. This heat comes from the Sun's rays.

RAIN PREDICTED, BUT WE'RE GETTING SOME FLYING IN WHILE IT'S CLEAR

THE SNOW IS GREAT FOR SKIING BUT TRANSPORTATION IS PROVING DIFFICULT

When the temperature is very low, instead of rain we have SLEET, HAIL or SNOW.

Weather worship

Across the world, people have worshipped weather gods. The Aztec Indians from Central America worshipped a sun god called Tezcatlipoca and a rain god called Tláloc. Some Indian tribes from North America still perform special rain dances (left), asking the spirits to send rain for their crops.

5

UP IN THE ATMOSPHERE

The atmosphere is made up of layers of air which surround the Earth. Nitrogen and oxygen are the main gases in the atmosphere. It also contains tiny amounts of other gases, dust and water vapour. Our weather is caused by changes in the atmosphere. Most of these changes happen in the layer of air that is closest to the Earth's surface – this layer is called the troposphere.

Air on the move

The air in the atmosphere is heated by the Sun's rays. Warm air weighs less than cold air and so it rises. The air above sinks down again to replace it. The force of air on the Earth is called air pressure.

The Earth's atmosphere

The different layers of the atmosphere (see right) reach up to about 1,600 km above the Earth's surface. Beyond the atmosphere is the beginning of space.

Most of our weather happens in the TROPOSPHERE. At the top of this layer is the tropopause, which forms the boundary between the troposphere and the next layer.

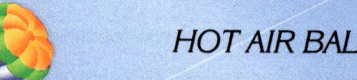

HOT AIR BALLOONS

EARTH

GLIDER

Making a hot air spiral

Colour a circle of thin card and draw a spiral onto it. You can decorate it with pictures of things that fly. Cut along the spiral to make a coil and attach a piece of string to the top. Hang your spiral above a warm radiator and watch it turn as the warm air from the radiator rises.

Weather balloons

Weather balloons are sent up into the atmosphere to record the weather conditions. They carry instruments which can measure the temperature, the air pressure, the amount of moisture in the air and the speed of the wind.

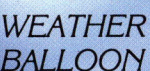

WEATHER BALLOON

Within the stratosphere there is a thin layer of gas called the OZONE LAYER. It takes in, or absorbs, the harmful rays from the Sun.

JET AIRCRAFT

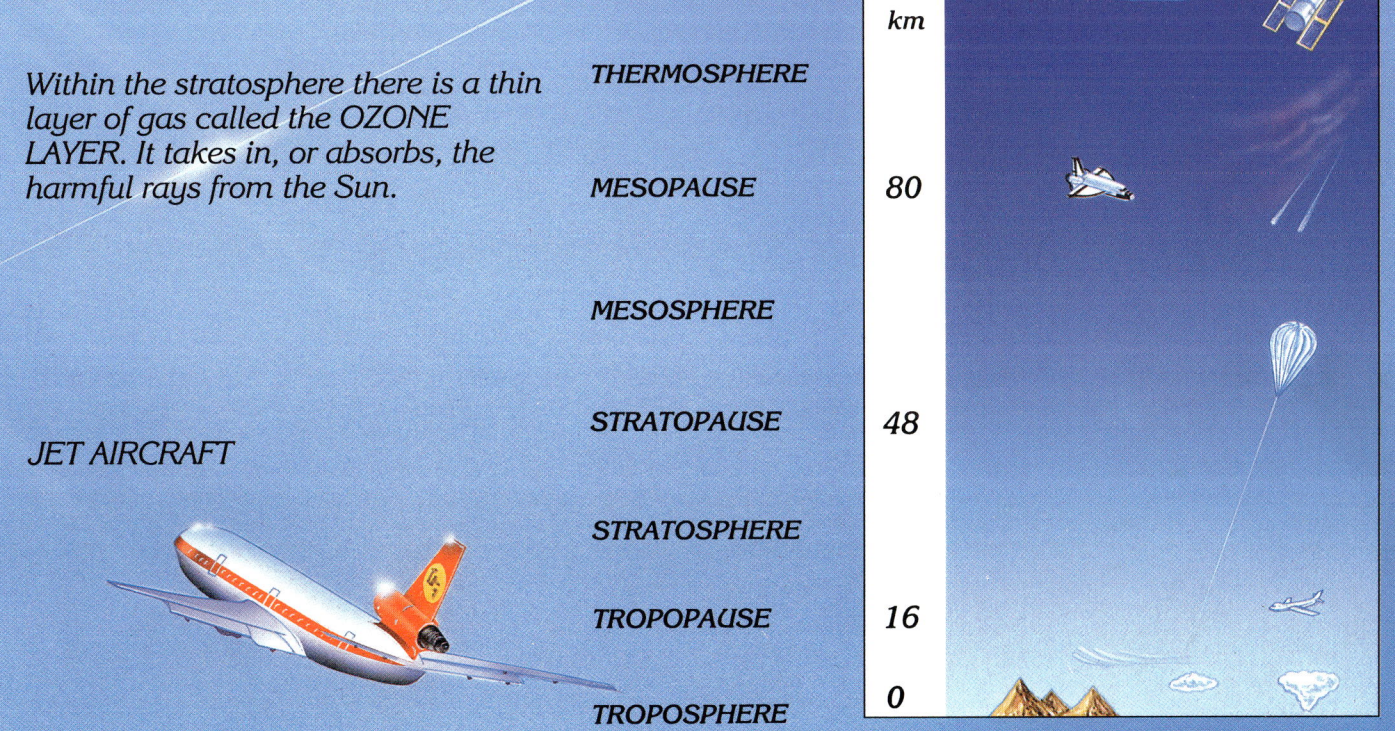

	km
THERMOSPHERE	
MESOPAUSE	80
MESOSPHERE	
STRATOPAUSE	48
STRATOSPHERE	
TROPOPAUSE	16
TROPOSPHERE	0

HOT AND COLD

MERCURY OR ALCOHOL

The heat from the Sun warms the Earth and the air. Some places on Earth receive more of the Sun's rays and so they are hotter. Places near the Equator are the hottest, while the North and South Poles are extremely cold. Here the rays from the Sun spread out and so they are much weaker.

Measuring the temperature

Temperature tells us how hot or cold something or someone is. We measure temperature with a thermometer. The most common ones have a glass tube filled with liquid alcohol or mercury. When the temperature increases, the liquid rises in the tube. A scale is marked (in degrees Celsius) on the outside.

Hot countries

In countries close to the Equator, the weather is nearly always hot because the Sun is almost directly overhead. To keep cool, people in hot countries wear loose, flowing, light-coloured clothes made of cool fabrics like cotton and linen.

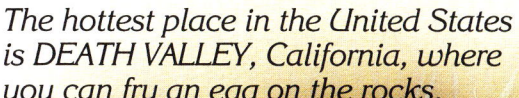

Hibernation

During very cold weather, some animals protect themselves by going to sleep. This is called hibernation. Dormice and ground squirrels eat lots of food first, for energy while they are asleep. Snakes hibernate underground, but bats choose caves or hollow trees for their sleep.

Cold countries

Near the North and South Poles, the Sun is low in the sky. Its rays are less powerful and bring less heat. The weather is cold, even in the summer. Some places have snow for about nine months each year. People living there keep warm by wearing thick heavy clothes made from wool and animal fur.

The INUIT people live near the Arctic Circle. They make their clothes from caribou or seal skins, which are very warm.

CLOUDY SKIES

A cloud is a mass of tiny droplets of water or crystals of ice. There are lots of different clouds in many shapes and colours. Some are fluffy and others spread across the sky. Cirrus clouds are high up in the sky, while stratus-cumulus clouds are low down. Clouds form when air in the atmosphere rises and then cools. At the same time the water vapour in the air changes into millions of tiny drops of water or ice.

Fog and mist

Fog is a mass of tiny drops of water. It touches the ground, often near the coast or high up in the hills, making it difficult to see. Mist is a thin form of fog.

WARM AIR COOLS

MOIST WARM AIR RISES

CLOUDS FORM

Making clouds

Running a hot bath makes white clouds appear as water vapour cools and turns into clouds of water drops. Make your own clouds by filling a plastic bottle with hot (not boiling) water. In a few minutes empty two-thirds of the water. Put an ice cube on the top of the bottle and watch your clouds form.

CIRRUS

STRATUS

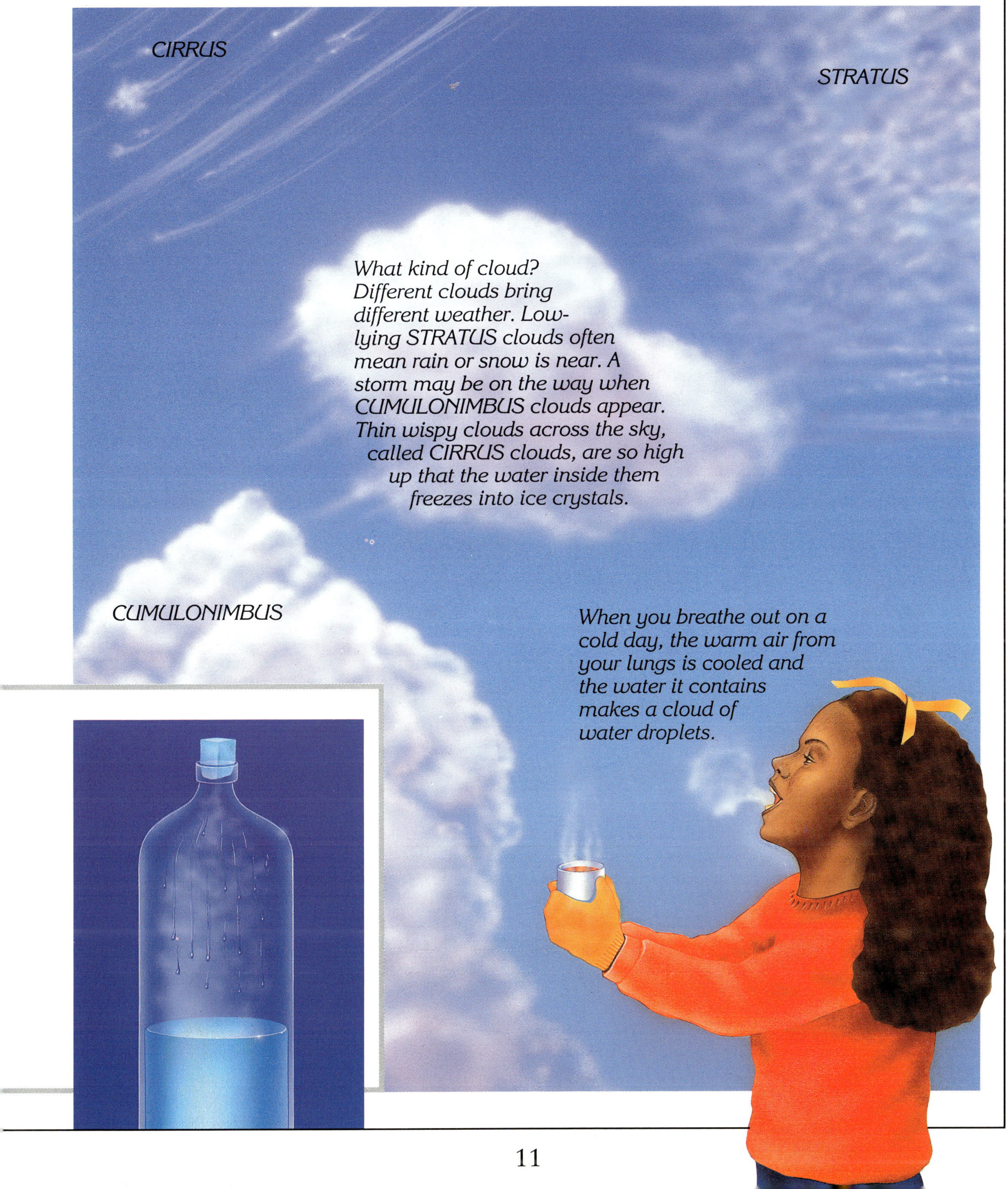

*What kind of cloud?
Different clouds bring different weather. Low-lying STRATUS clouds often mean rain or snow is near. A storm may be on the way when CUMULONIMBUS clouds appear. Thin wispy clouds across the sky, called CIRRUS clouds, are so high up that the water inside them freezes into ice crystals.*

CUMULONIMBUS

When you breathe out on a cold day, the warm air from your lungs is cooled and the water it contains makes a cloud of water droplets.

WINDY WEATHER

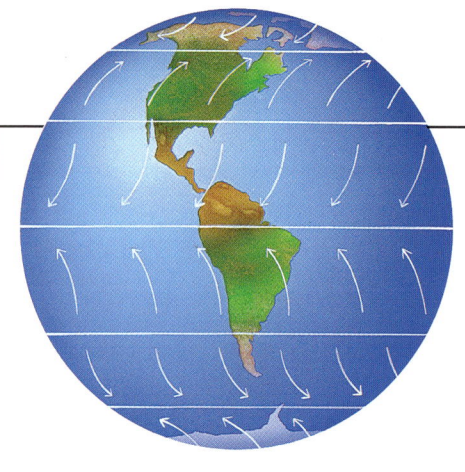

The world's winds

Winds move in six main bands (above). Many have special names such as trade winds. They were used by sailors long ago, when trade between different countries was transported by sea.

Winds can change a hot day into a cool one, or blow away clouds on a rainy day so that the weather becomes sunny. Winds can blow as a gentle breeze, or be strong enough to blow down trees and buildings. When air in the atmosphere moves across the Earth's surface it causes winds. Air movement happens when heated air rises and is replaced by cooler air from another area (see page 6).

Wind power, first used for windmills to grind corn, now powers WIND TURBINES (left) to generate electricity.

Beaufort Scale

The strength of wind is described using a scale called the Beaufort Wind Scale, named after a British admiral Sir Francis Beaufort, who invented it. The scale is from 0 (calm) up to 12 (hurricane).

3
GENTLE
BREEZE

5
FRESH
BREEZE

Build a weather vane

An instrument used to measure wind speed is called an anemometer. A wind vane (or weather vane) tells us the direction of the wind. You can make your own weather vane with the help of an adult. Nail together two strips of wood to make a cross. Then glue a plastic cup onto each point, and paint one of the cups brightly. Make a hole in the middle of the cross and push a garden cane through it. Drop the cane into a bamboo tube pushed into the ground. On a windy day, count how many times in, say, 30 seconds the coloured cup spins past the marker on the front. Do the same on other days and compare your results. You can add a wind vane made from balsa wood to the top of the cane.

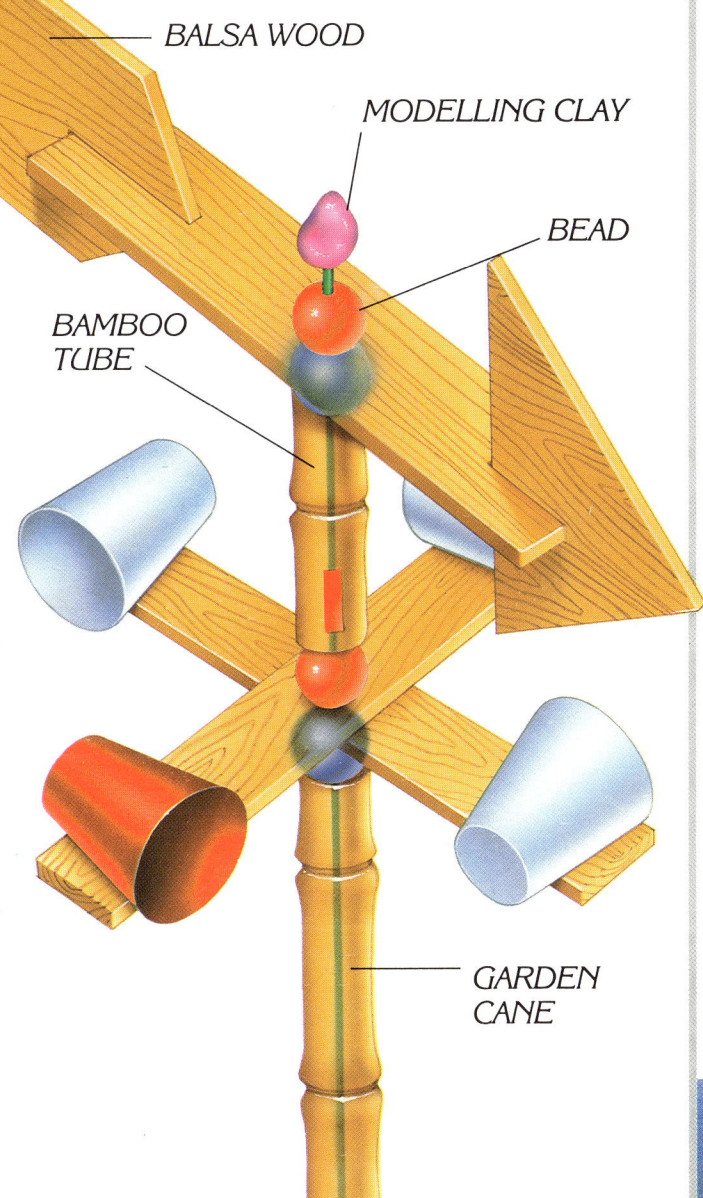

BALSA WOOD

MODELLING CLAY

BEAD

BAMBOO TUBE

GARDEN CANE

7 MODERATE GALE

10 WHOLE GALE

12 HURRICANE

RAINY DAYS

Water is always on the move – from the oceans and rivers up into the air, onto the land and back into the sea. This is called the water cycle. Heat from the Sun warms the water on Earth and some of it becomes water vapour. This rises, cools and turns into water droplets. Eventually they become large and heavy and fall as rain, sleet or snow.

Rainbows

Rainbows appear when the sun shines after rain. Sunlight is a mixture of colours. As it shines on raindrops, they split the sunlight into its separate colours: red, orange, yellow, green, blue, indigo and violet.

1 Heat from the Sun's rays warms the water so that it turns into water vapour, or EVAPORATES.

The HOPI INDIANS of North America dance with live snakes in their mouths, asking their gods to send rain.

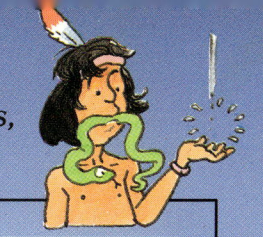

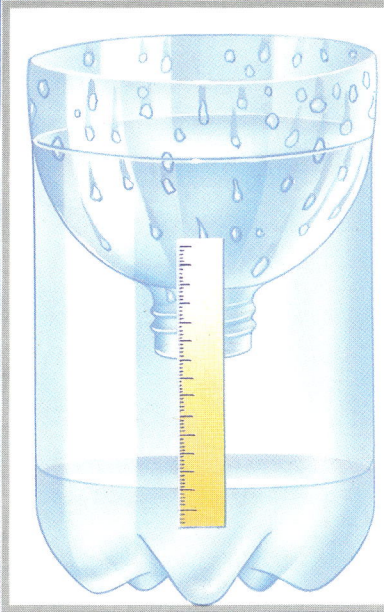

Measuring rain

A rain gauge is an instrument for measuring rainfall. Cut the top off a plastic bottle and put it upside down in the bottom half. Tape a ruler to the side (in millimetres) as a scale. Put the gauge in a hole outdoors, with the top above ground level. Find out the daily or weekly rainfall where you live.

2 The warm damp air rises and cools. Finally it turns back into water droplets, or CONDENSES, and clouds form.

3 The droplets inside the clouds become larger and heavier and fall to the ground as RAIN.

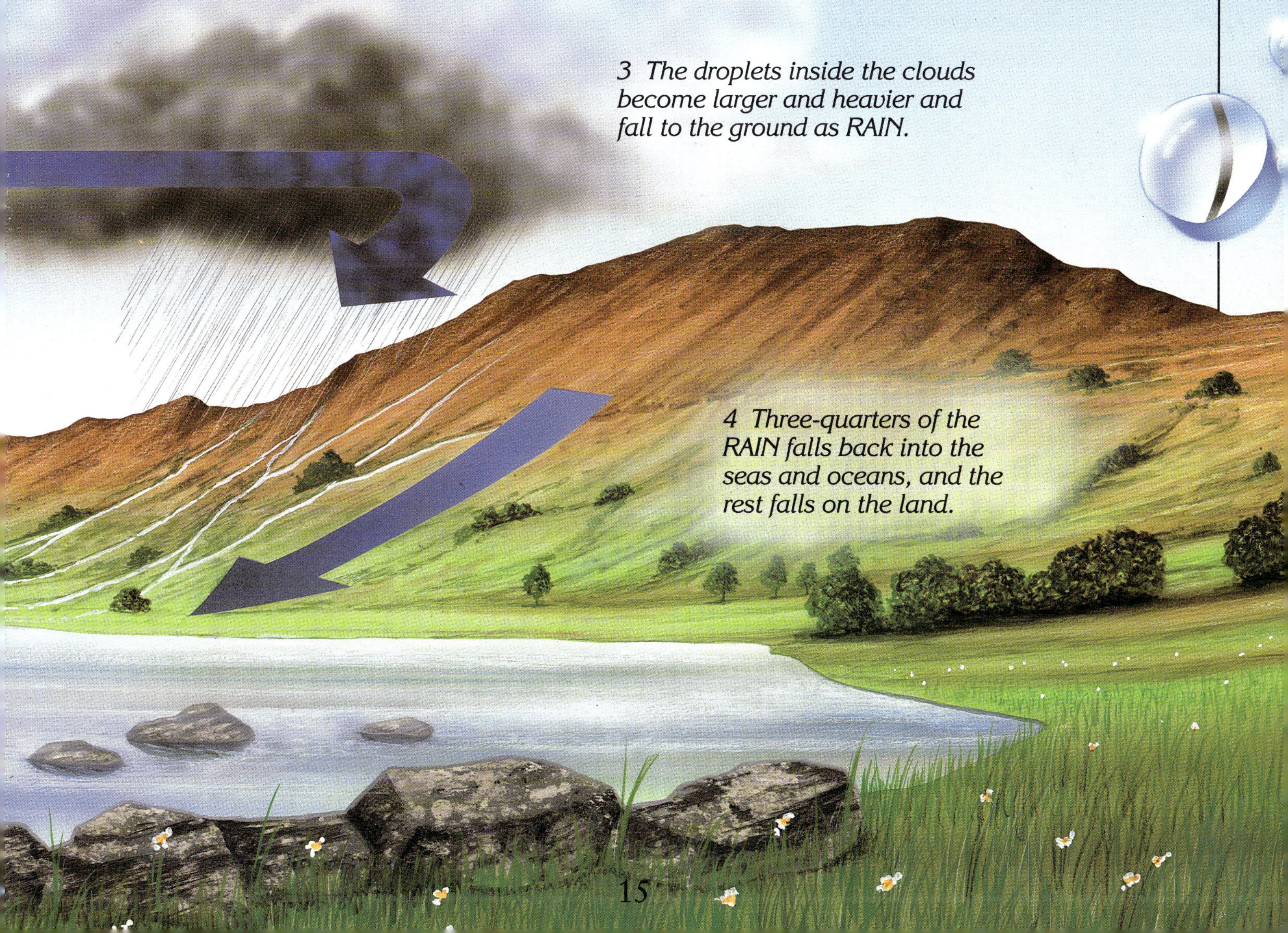

4 Three-quarters of the RAIN falls back into the seas and oceans, and the rest falls on the land.

FROST, ICE AND SNOW

Water freezes below 0 degrees Celcius and becomes ice. Frost, sleet, snow and hail are forms of ice. High in the air, water droplets freeze in the clouds to form snow. The frozen drops become crystals of ice which bump into each other and stick together to become snowflakes. You need to melt 30 cm of fluffy snow to get just 1 cm of water.

Frost

When ice crystals appear in patterns on windows or on grass and plants, we say there has been a frost. You usually find a frost in the morning after a cold clear night. Frost can damage or even kill some kinds of plants.

Winter SNOW in countries such as the USA, Russia and Sweden can be heavy and make travel to school or work difficult.

Snow shapes

Although all snowflakes have six sides, no two flakes are alike. Some snowflakes contain more than 100 ice crystals, but others are tiny and have only a handful of crystals. Some snowflakes are star-shaped and some are like flat needles of ice. A snowflake can change its shape as it falls if the air temperature either drops or rises.

Why do pipes burst?

When the weather is very cold, the water inside the pipes may freeze and turn to ice. Ice takes up more space than water and as it slowly expands it may sometimes burst the pipe. When the ice finally melts, water pours out through the burst pipe. This can be seen using a plastic bottle filled with water then frozen. The expanding water will crack the bottle.

What is hail?

Hail is like rain that falls as hard round lumps of ice, or hailstones. Most are small, but some are bigger than tennis balls. They can break windows and even dent cars. Inside storm clouds, frozen raindrops are thrown up and down by the air. A layer of ice forms around the raindrop each time it is tossed up and down inside the cloud until finally a hailstone is formed.

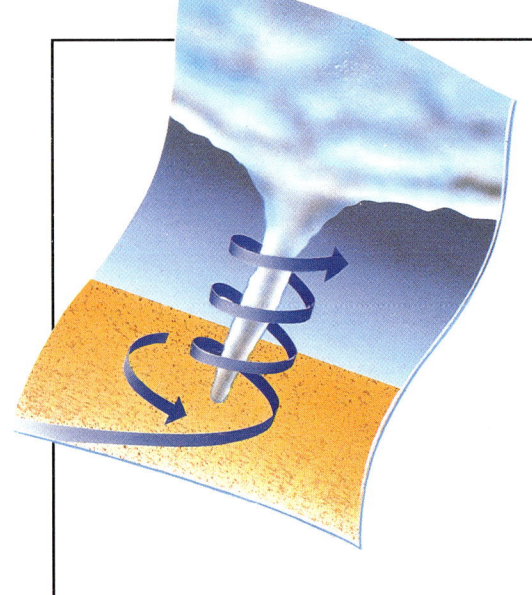

Storms are when heavy rain and strong winds are often accompanied by thunder and lightning. In tropical countries they can cause terrible damage. Severe storms are called hurricanes over the Atlantic Ocean and West Indies. Elsewhere they are known as typhoons or cyclones.

Cyclones

Small thunderstorms last hours, but cyclones can rage for weeks, with winds of up to 290 km per hour. In Bangladesh, many people live on the coast. When a cyclone struck in 1991, 250,000 people died and millions lost their homes.

DROUGHT is another kind of extreme weather, when no rain falls for days, weeks or even years on end. During a severe drought, crops and farm animals die, and people may go hungry.

Hurricanes and tornadoes

Hurricanes are powerful storms, bringing swirling winds that start in an area of extreme low pressure. At the centre of a hurricane is a calm area called the "eye", which can be as wide as 40 kilometres. Each year, hurricanes are named in alphabetical order; the first one is given a name beginning with "A", such as Alicia, the second one beginning with "B", and so on. A tornado is a funnel of violently swirling air stretching from the bottom of a thundercloud to the ground.

Storm gods

For thousands of years, people believed in storm gods. Raijin (below), was the Japanese spirit of thunder and people believed that thunder was the sound of Raijin beating on his ring of drums. Thunder is really the noise made by gases in the air expanding with the heat of sudden lightening.

WHAT IS CLIMATE?

Weather changes but local climate does not. Climate is an area's average weather over a long period. Sun and little rainfall is a desert climate. Hot dry summers and cool wet winters are a Mediterranean climate. Hot weather all year with a dry season and a rainy season, is a tropical climate.

The Poles
At the Poles the weather is always cold and mostly dry, although it does warm up a little during the summer.

Deserts
In a desert climate, it is very hot in the day but cooler at night. Rainfall is very low.

Highlands
Mountains and highlands have a cool, wet climate, often with snow.

The seasons

Many places have four seasons (below). As the Earth moves around the Sun, some places have lots of sun and others little. Between March and September the northern half of the world gets more sun and has spring and summer, while in the south it is autumn and winter. From September to March the reverse is true.

| *WINTER* | *SPRING* | *SUMMER* | *AUTUMN* |

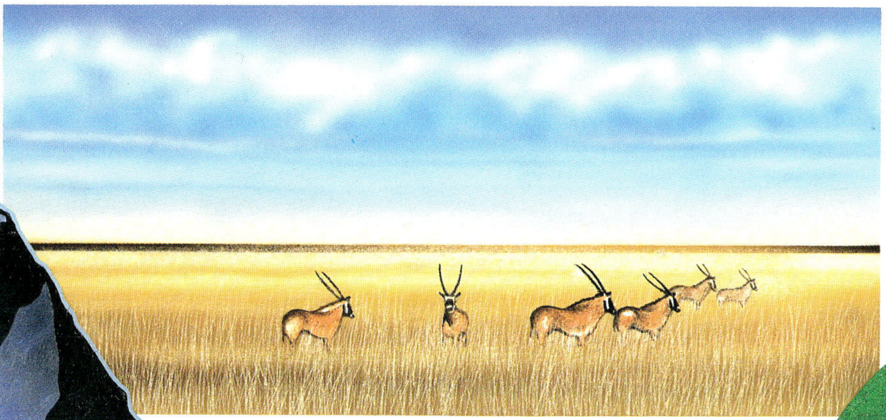

Grasslands

Grasslands, which cover over a quarter of the Earth's surface, have hot dry summers and long cold winters.

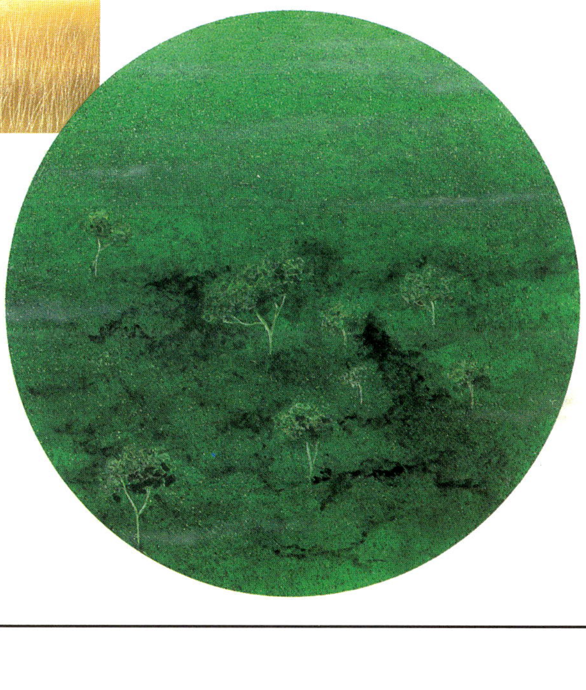

Rainforests

The tropical wet climate in the rainforests means hot rainy weather all year round.

LIVING WITH THE WEATHER

Life in hot places

Some desert animals, like the kangaroo rat, avoid hot sun by hiding underground until the cool of night, when they feed. Larger animals, like camels and deer, stay in the shade of trees or rocks. Cactus plants (above) provide food and water for insects and other small desert animals.

Weather and climate affect our homes, food, animals and plants. In a desert climate, houses are built to keep out hot sun, but in a temperate climate houses are designed to keep out the cold winter weather. People have a way of life that suits their climate. Animals also adapt to a particular kind of weather. Desert animals, for example, can survive for a long time without water.

OWL

MULE DEER

KIT FOX

KANGAROO RAT

LIZARD

Each year the ARCTIC TERN flies up to 35,000 km from one end of the world to the other, and back again to find food.

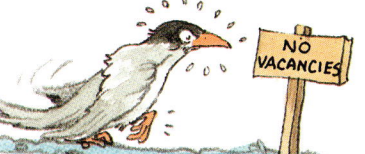

What kind of house?

People build houses to protect themselves from the weather. In the rainforest, huts have thatched roofs so the rain runs off easily. Homes in flood areas are often on stilts above ground. Bedouins have cool shady tents in the desert, while the Mongols in Asia live in felt-covered tents, called yurts, which protect them from both cold and heat.

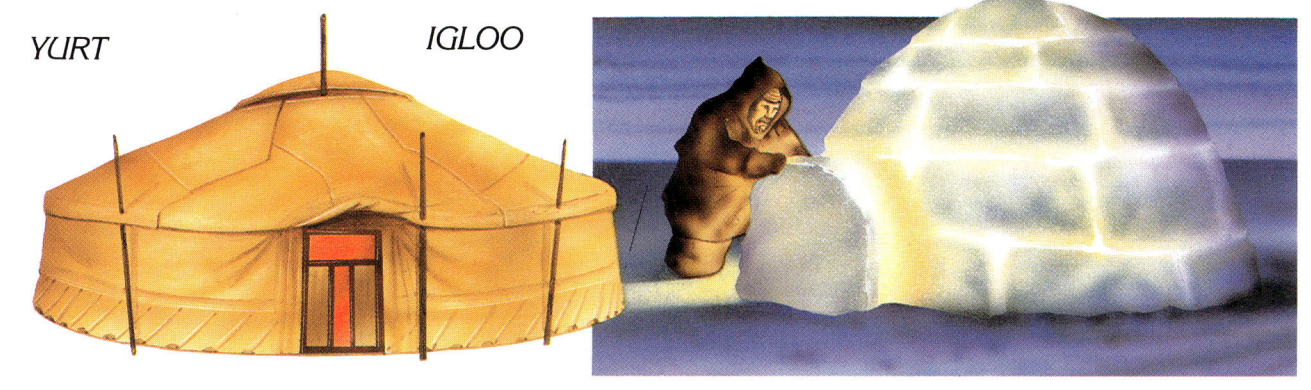

YURT

IGLOO

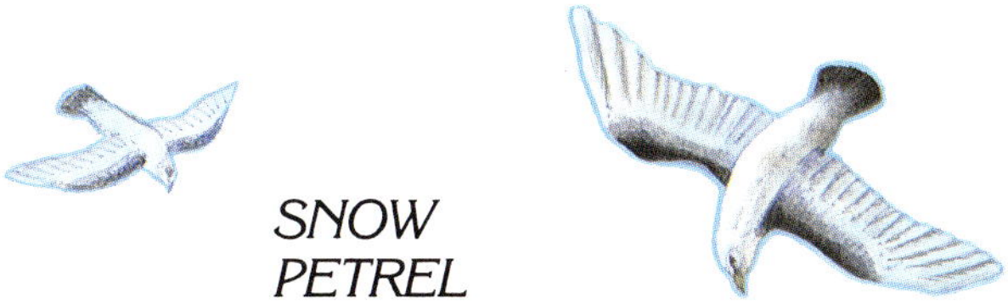

SNOW PETREL

Surviving the cold

Few animals can survive in polar regions. Many of these animals, such as penguins and seals, have extra layers of fat for warmth. In some seals this fatty layer can be 15 cm thick. The fat helps the animals to survive without food. Some creatures, like whales and birds, escape the coldest weather by travelling to warmer areas.

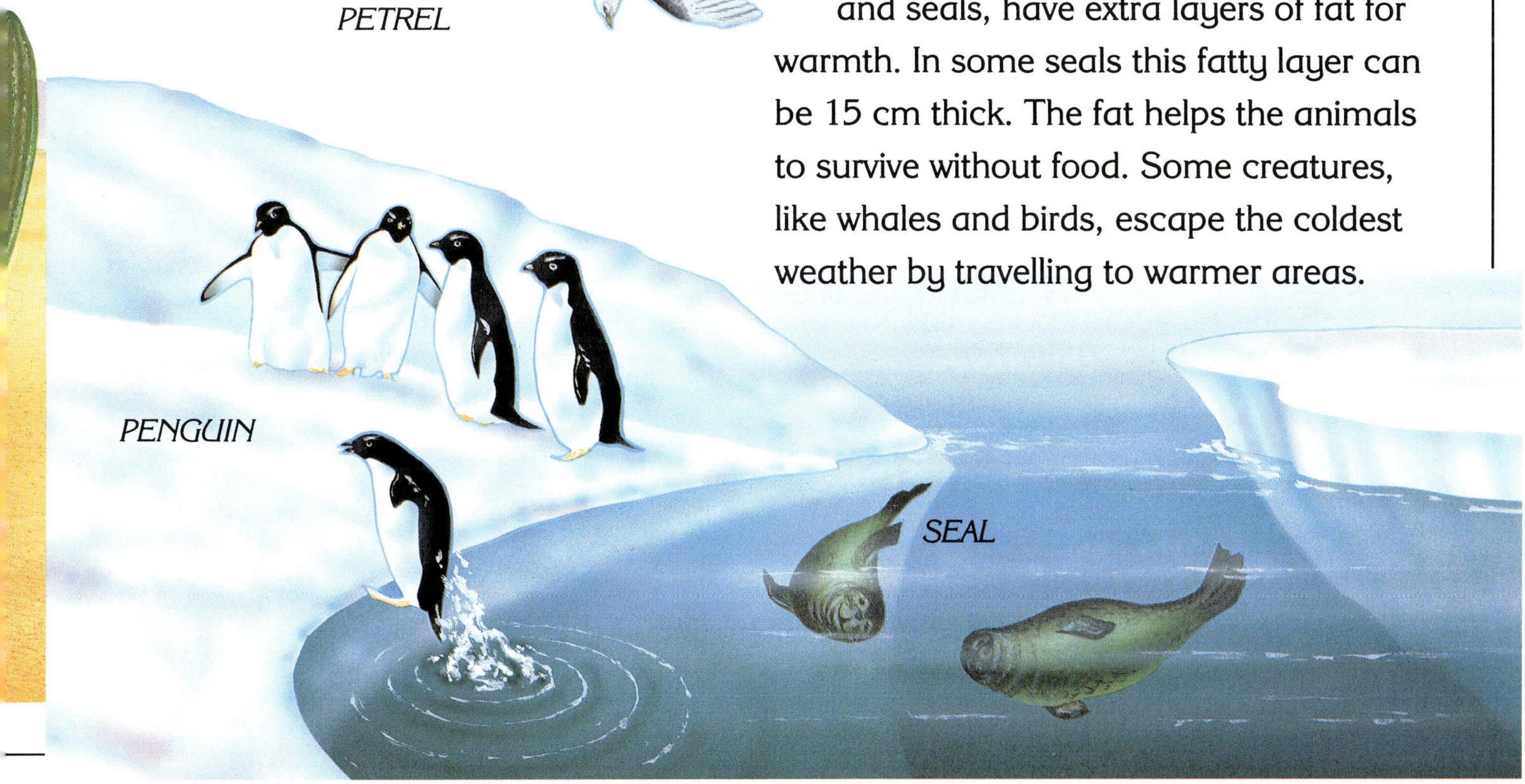

PENGUIN

SEAL

UV RAYS

OZONE HOLE

CHANGING THE WEATHER

People think the world's weather is changing. Human beings are filling the atmosphere with harmful gases by burning fuels in cars and factories. These gases may be increasing world temperatures; this increase is called global warming. It could affect winds and rainfall as well. Scientists think some parts of the world may have droughts if this "warming" continues.

The ozone hole
There is a thin area, or "hole", in the ozone layer above Antarctica. This was caused by chemicals, called CFCs (chlorofluorocarbons), which humans have added to the atmosphere.

VOLCANOES may make our weather cooler, because the dust from an erupting volcano blocks out some of the Sun's rays.

Beware of the sunshine
High up above the Earth's surface, a layer of ozone gas protects us from the Sun's damaging rays. These harmful rays are called ultraviolet rays (UV rays). As the ozone layer becomes thinner, or even disappears altogether in places (see above left), more and more sunshine reaches us on Earth. Powerful UV rays can cause sunburn and serious diseases like skin cancer.

Some scientists predict that by the year 2030, RISING SEA-LEVELS could cover New York's Statue of Liberty.

Ice ages

Through time the world climate has changed. There have been several different Ice Ages – most recently around 2 million years ago. Mammoths and woolly rhinoceroses roamed the land but disappeared forever when the ice sheets melted.

A carving of a BISON which lived during the Ice Age.

When we burn FUELS such as coal, oil and gas, the atmosphere fills up with harmful carbon dioxide and other gases which could destroy the ozone layer.

WEATHER FORECASTS

Many people need to know what the weather will be like – tomorrow, next week or even next month. The weather is very important to fishermen, airline pilots, farmers, sports players and so on. People who study the weather are called meteorologists. They measure the temperature, the rainfall, the speed and direction of the wind. They also receive information from weather stations on land, at sea, up in the air and even up in space. Meteorologists use this information to make a weather forecast, which tells us what kind of weather we can expect in the future.

SATELLITES in space send back pictures of the Earth to weather stations on the ground.

WEATHER MAP SYMBOLS

SUNNY   PARTLY CLOUDY   CLOUDY

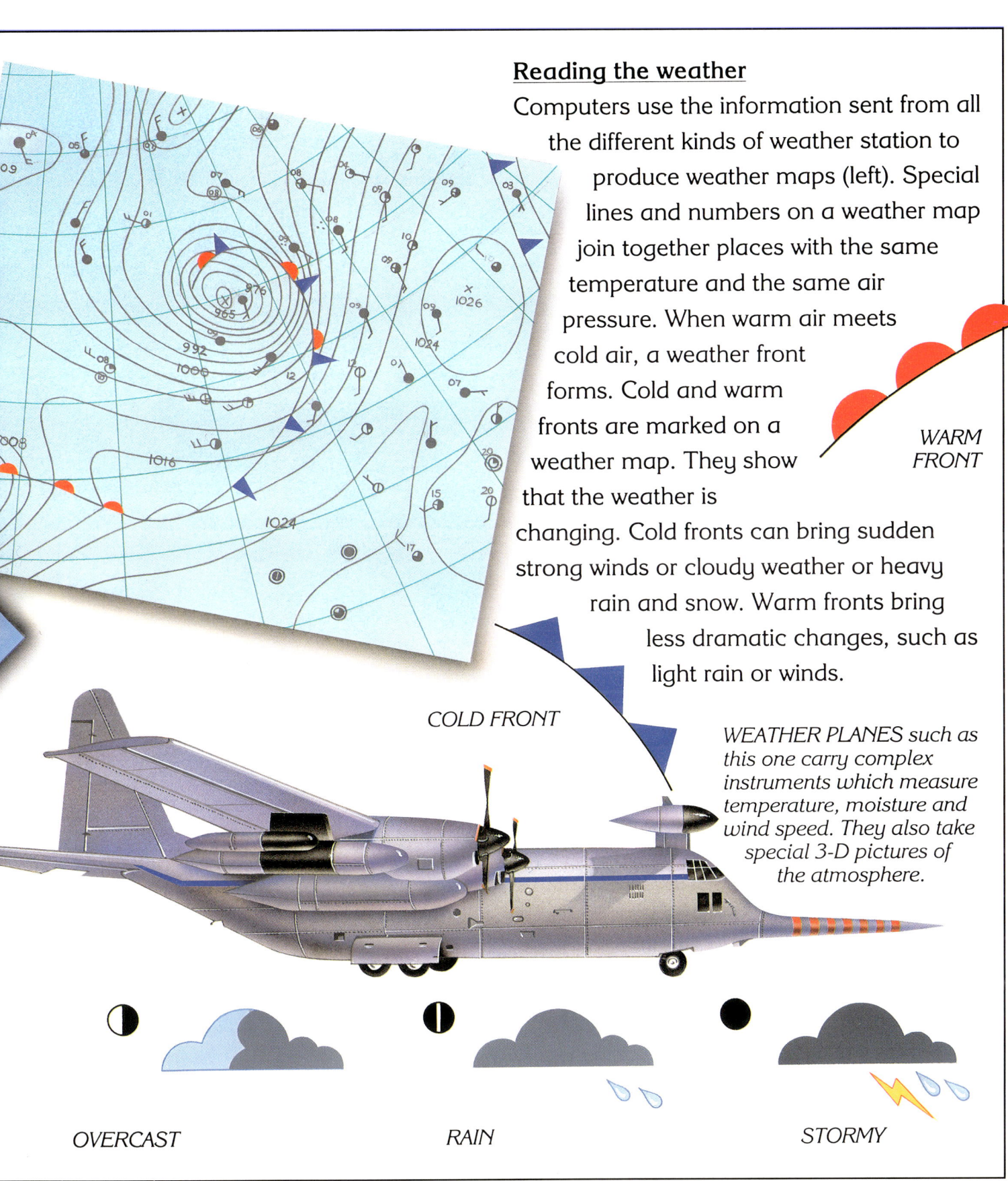

Reading the weather

Computers use the information sent from all the different kinds of weather station to produce weather maps (left). Special lines and numbers on a weather map join together places with the same temperature and the same air pressure. When warm air meets cold air, a weather front forms. Cold and warm fronts are marked on a weather map. They show that the weather is changing. Cold fronts can bring sudden strong winds or cloudy weather or heavy rain and snow. Warm fronts bring less dramatic changes, such as light rain or winds.

WARM FRONT

COLD FRONT

WEATHER PLANES such as this one carry complex instruments which measure temperature, moisture and wind speed. They also take special 3-D pictures of the atmosphere.

OVERCAST

RAIN

STORMY

WEATHER DIARY

Keep a weather diary to note information and observations about the weather where you live. You can use your diary as a record of the weather during the year. You can also try to predict the weather tomorrow, or next week. Record the weather for one day at least once a week. Make observations at three different times during the day. Use your own symbols for different weather conditions. As well as temperature and rainfall, note cloud types, the amount of cloud cover, wind direction, mist or fog, the hours of sunshine and so on.

Take photos of types of cloud for your weather diary.

Use your rain gauge to keep a record of the weekly and monthly rainfall.

Mon 7th JANUARY
BRIGHT START
TEMP 3°C

2:00 pm
CLOUD GATHERING

NATURE NOTES:-
PINE CONES
OPENING

7.00 pm OVERCAST
RAIN
7°C TEMP
RAINFALL:-
1mm
DARK AT

Use the weather instruments shown in this book to help you make a weather diary. If you have no garden, you can stand your weather vane in a garden pot on any flat surface outdoors.

Place your thermometer in a shady place.

Nature's reporters

The changes in certain plants can indicate different weather conditions. The scales of pine cones open up in dry weather but close up tightly when the air is damp, to keep the seeds inside dry. The white poplar tree shows the underside of its leaves when rain is approaching.

"Red sky at night, shepherd's delight,
Red sky in the morning, shepherd's warning."
"Rain before seven
Fine before eleven."
"The north wind doth blow
And we shall have snow."
"One swallow doesn't make a summer."

If rain is on the way, this SEAWEED swells and feels damp.

The flowers of the MORNING GLORY plant open up in fine or sunny weather.

MORE AMAZING FACTS

The usually hot desert climate of Syria had an unexpected change in 1988 when snow fell.

An unexpected gale drove Captain Cook towards what was then the undiscovered coast of Australia.

The Empire State building in New York was struck by lightning 48 times in one day.

On Mt Wai-ale'-ale' in Hawaii it rains for up to 350 days each year.

On 23 November 1981, there were 58 separate tornadoes across England and Wales.

The driest place in the world is in the Atacam desert, Chile. It did not rain for 400 years until 1971.

At Commonwealth Bay in Antarctica, the world's windiest place, the wind blows at speeds of up to 320 km per hour.

GLOSSARY

AIR PRESSURE The weight of the air in the atmosphere pressing down on the Earth's surface.

ANEMOMETER An instrument that is used to measure the speed of the wind.

ATMOSPHERE The layers of air that surround the Earth.

CLIMATE The average weather in a particular area of the world over a long period of time.

CONDENSE To cool down and change from a gas, such as water vapour, to a liquid.

CYCLONE A kind of hurricane.

DROUGHT Little or no rainfall for a long period of time.

EQUATOR An imaginary line around the centre of the Earth.

EVAPORATE The process in which a liquid changes to a gas.

FRONT An area where warm air meets cold air.

GLOBAL WARMING The gradual warming-up of the Earth.

HAIL Large lumps of frozen rain.

HIBERNATION A deep winter sleep which helps certain animals to survive the cold weather.

HURRICANE A powerful swirling storm with high winds.

ICE AGE A time in the past when large areas of the Earth were covered in ice.

METEOROLOGIST A person who studies the weather.

OZONE HOLE A thin patch in the ozone layer that surrounds the Earth.

OZONE LAYER A layer of ozone gas in the atmosphere which protects the Earth from the Sun's harmful rays.

SLEET Tiny pieces of ice that are made from frozen raindrops.

TORNADO A violent funnel-shaped storm which is similar to a cyclone.

INDEX